WORSHIP TOGE com

your premiere online destination for worship resources

www.worshiptogether.com

SONGBOOK 3.0

Songbook 3.0

Index of Songs by Key (Appendix A)
Index of Songs by Tempo (Appendix B)
Index of Songs by Project (Appendix C)

1

All Creation

Words and Music by
BRIAN DOERKSEN and STEVE MITCHINSON

ev - 'ry rhy - thm we___ thank You   for Your___ love.___
ev - 'ry sea - son we___ thank You,   for Your___ love.___

D.S. al Fine

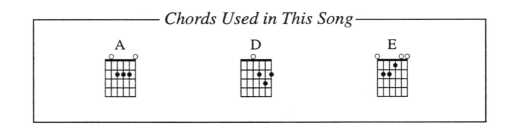

Chords Used in This Song

A   D   E

All That I Need

Words and Music by
VICKY BEECHING

Chords Used in This Song

E   E2/D#   C#m7   A2   B

C2   D   Bsus   G#m7   F#m7

All Who Are Thirsty

Words and Music by
BRENTON BROWN and GLENN ROBERTSON

America

Words and Music by
CHRIS TOMLIN, J.D. WALT
and JACK PARKER

5 At All Times

Words and Music by
VICKY BEECHING

Awaken the Dawn

Capo 1 (E)

Words and Music by
STUART GARRARD

Chords Used in This Song

Be the Centre

Words and Music by
MICHAEL FRYE

⊕ CODA

be my light. Je - sus.

Je - sus.

Chords Used in This Song

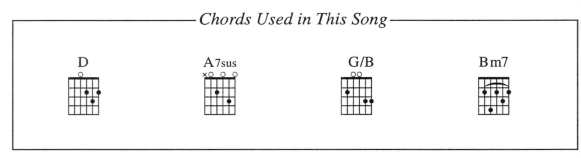

D   A7sus   G/B   Bm7

Better Is One Day

Words and Music by
MATT REDMAN

With a strong beat

one   day___   than thou - sands   else - where.   Bet - ter is

one   day,___   bet - ter is   one   day,___   bet - ter is

D.S. al CODA %

one   day___   than thou - sands   else - where.___   Bet - ter is

CODA

else - where.___

— *Chords Used in This Song* —

Eno3   A2   Bsus   A/C#   E/G#   C#m7   B   F#m7
7fr.   2fr.   4fr.

9

Break Our Hearts

Words and Music by
BILLY JAMES FOOTE

We cry out, we need Your help; come back to our land. We con- fess, we've lived in sin. Please show Your pow- er once a- gain.

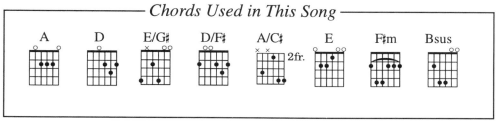

Chords Used in This Song

A   D   E/G♯   D/F♯   A/C♯   E   F♯m   Bsus

10   Breathe

Words and Music by
MARIE BARNETT

With emotion

This is— the air— I breathe,—

this is— the air— I breathe,—

Your ho - ly pres - ence

liv - ing   in me.—   And

CODA

I'm lost with-out___ You,___

I'm lost with-out___ You.___

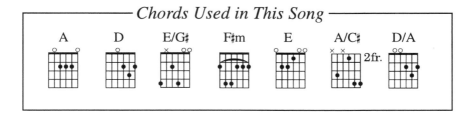

11
Child of God

Words and Music by
KATHRYN SCOTT

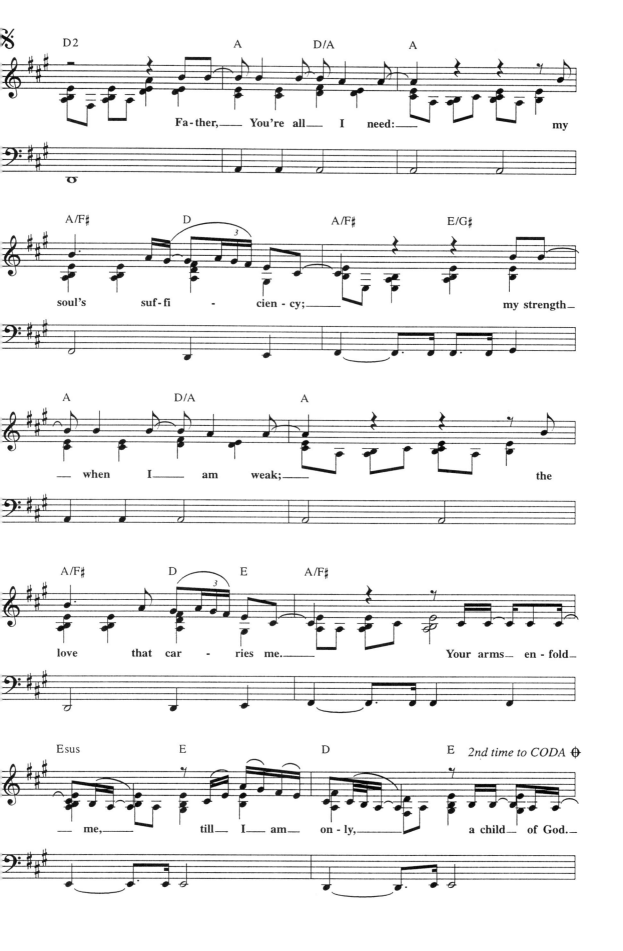

D | Esus | E | A

fa-ther - ing me.

CODA

A | Esus | E

Your arms— en - fold—— me,——— till— I— am—

D | E | A

on - ly,———— a child— of God.

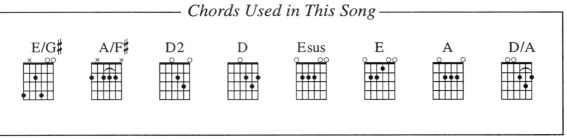

--- *Chords Used in This Song* ---

E/G♯   A/F♯   D2   D   Esus   E   A   D/A

Devotion

**Words and Music by
KATHRYN SCOTT**

Did You Feel the Mountains Tremble?

Words and Music by
MARTIN SMITH

Everything

Words and Music by
MARTIN SMITH
and STUART GARRARD

15 The Father's Song

Words and Music by
MATT REDMAN

Capo 1 (D)

Tenderly

I have heard so man-y songs, lis-tened to a thou-sand tongues, but there is one that sounds a-bove them all:___ The Fa-ther's song, the Fa-ther's love,

For Me

Words and Music by
NIGEL BRIGGS

Give Us Clean Hands

Prayerfully

Words and Music by
CHARLIE HALL

God, You Are My God

Moderate rock beat

Words and Music by
STUART GARRARD

I live.———　　　　　　　　　　　　　　So, I will

praise You———　　　　　　　　　as long as　I live.———

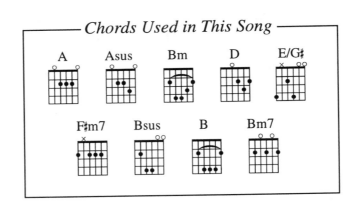

Chords Used in This Song

A　　Asus　　Bm　　D　　E/G♯

F♯m7　　Bsus　　B　　Bm7

God's Romance

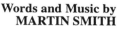

Words and Music by
MARTIN SMITH

With a driving beat

1. There's a song that ev-'ry-one___ can sing; there's a
(2. There's a) song that ev-'ry-one___ can sing; there's a

prayer that ev-'ry-one___ can bring. Feel___ the
race that ev-'ry-one___ can win. Leave___ your

mu - sic, 'cause___ it's time to
sad - ness; it's___ our time to

dance.
dance.

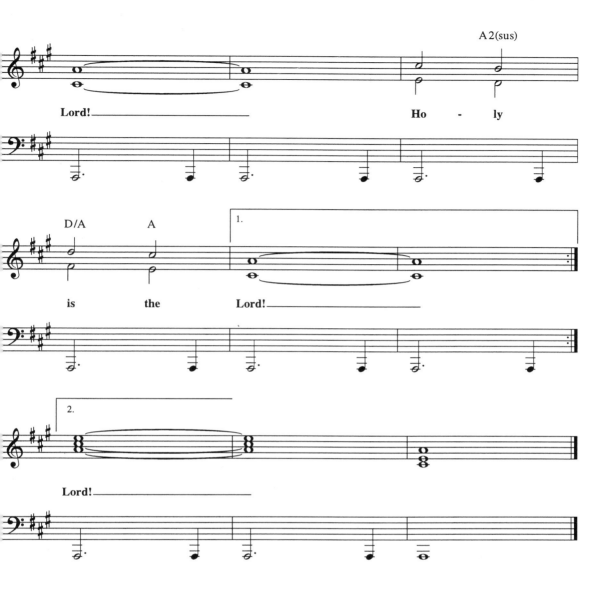

Lord!_____ Ho - ly

is the Lord!_____

1.

2.

Lord!_____

Chords Used in This Song

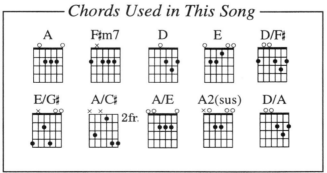

A   F#m7   D   E   D/F#

E/G#   A/C#   A/E   A2(sus)   D/A

20

Grace Flows Down

Words and Music by
DAVID BELL, LOUIE GIGLIO
and ROD PAGAENT

Hallelujah
(Your Love Is Amazing)

22

Hang on to You

Words and Music by
MARTIN SMITH

1. And I'll hang on to You,_____ 'cause You're strong-
(2. And Your love, it is) true._____ I feel strong-

-er and You keep____ me from fall-
-er and I'm hap - py to know

ing. And You bright - en the world_____ with Your beau-
You. 'Cause You shine like the sun,_____ and You're brigh-

-ty. Keep me clos - er; I'm call -
-ter than the dark - ness that's fall -

ho - ly___ face,___ in___ Your

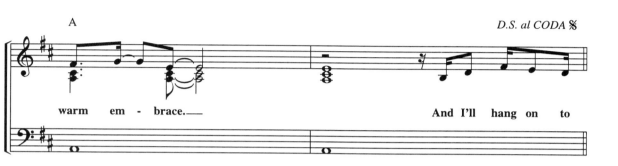

warm em - brace.___ And I'll hang on to

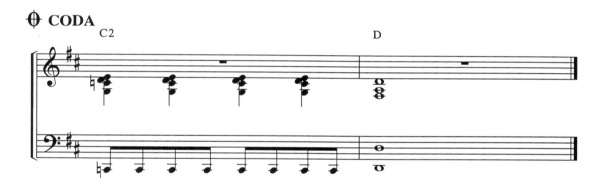

CODA

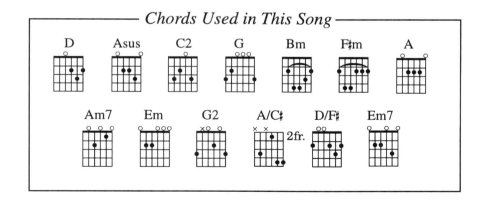

Chords Used in This Song

23

The Heart of Worship
(When the Music Fades)

Words and Music by
MATT REDMAN

Steadily

1. When the mu-sic fades,___ all is stripped a-way,___
2. King of end-less worth,___ no one could ex-press___

and I sim-ply come;___
how much You de-serve.___

long-ing just to bring___ some-thing that's of worth___
Though I'm weak and poor,___ all I have is Yours,___

that will bless Your heart.___
ev-'ry sin-gle breath.___

Chords Used in This Song

D2   A2   Em7   Asus   D/F♯   A2/C♯   G   A7sus

Holy Moment

24

Words and Music by
MATT REDMAN

Moderate rock beat

1. As we come___ to-day,___ we re-mind___ our-selves___ of what
2. Lord, with con - fi-dence___ we come___ be-fore___ Your throne___

___ we do;___ that these songs___
of grace.___ Not that we___

___ are not___ just songs,___ but signs___ of love___
de - serve___ to come,___ but You___ have paid___

___ for You.___ This is a
___ the way.___ You are the

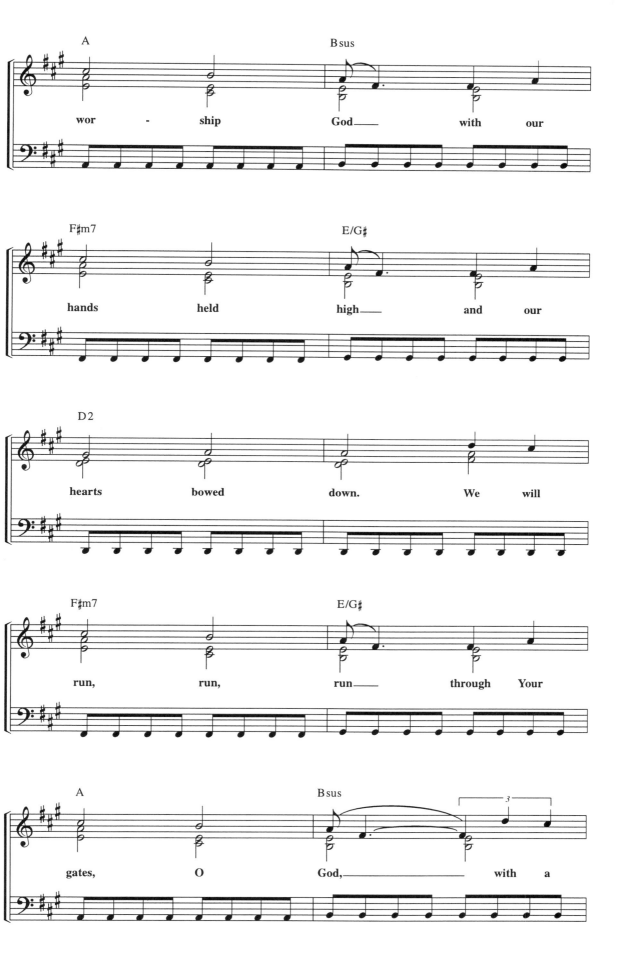

shout of love, with a

shout of love.

2. Lord, with con -

Chords Used in This Song

F#m7   E/G#   A   D   Bsus   D2

25

Holy Roar

Words and Music by
NATHAN and CHRISTY NOCKELS

Trees of life are bloom-ing, and

Your word plants the seed and we feel it

grow-ing, yeah. Your

kind-ness lead-ing to re-pen-tance, And

26

Holy Visitation
(Between Porch and Altar)

Words and Music by
CHARLIE HALL

Moderately

Sound the a-larm,_____ gath-er the peo-ple,_____ gath-er the el-ders, let the min-is-ters wail._____ God, take back the years_____ that the en-e-my's sto-len._____ Lord, You are com-ing;_____ Ho-ly Vis-i-

27

Humble King

**Words and Music by
BRENTON BROWN**

O kneel me down a-gain, here at Your feet;

show me how much You love hu - mil - i -

-ty. Oh, Spir - it, be the star

that leads me to the hum - ble

28

Hungry
(Falling on My Knees)

Words and Music by
KATHRYN SCOTT

1. Hun - gry, I come to You, for I know You sa - tis - fy.
2. Bro - ken, I run to You, for Your arms are o - pen wide;

I am emp - ty, but I know Your love
I am wea - ry, but I know Your touch

does not run dry. So I wait for You.
re - stores my life. So I wait for You.

So I wait for You. I'm fall -

29

I Could Sing of Your Love Forever

Words and Music by
MARTIN SMITH

Capo 3 (D)

Moderately

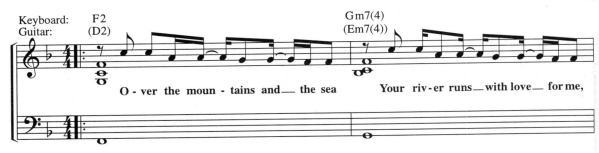

Keyboard: F2
Guitar: (D2)   Gm7(4)
(Em7(4))

O - ver the moun - tains and — the sea   Your riv-er runs — with love — for me,

Bb2
(G2)   Csus
(Asus)

and I will o - pen up my heart, —— and let the Heal - er set — me free.

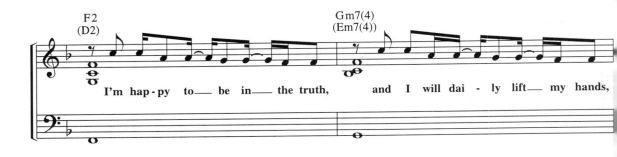

F2
(D2)   Gm7(4)
(Em7(4))

I'm hap-py to — be in — the truth,   and I will dai - ly lift — my hands,

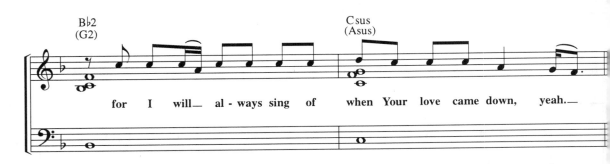

Bb2
(G2)   Csus
(Asus)

for I will — al - ways sing of   when Your love came down, yeah. —

it's fool-ish - ness,— I know.—

But when the world— has seen the light, they will dance—

— with joy— like we're danc - ing now.—

D.S. al CODA %

CODA

Chords Used in This Song

D2   Em7(4)   G2   Asus   Em7   D/F♯   G   A

I Fix My Eyes on You

30

With a driving beat ♩ = 100

Words and Music by
PAUL OAKLEY

1. I fix my eyes on You,⸺ on the things⸺ un - seen,⸺ on the things⸺ a - bove,⸺ on e - ter - ni - ty. I set my
2. I live my life for You⸺ as I walk⸺ by faith⸺ in the works⸺ You have⸺ pre - pared for me. I run this
3. I'll be a fool for You.⸺ As I car - ry the cross,⸺ help me walk⸺ in love⸺ and⸺ pur - i - ty. So let Your

I Have Come to Love You

Words and Music by
MARTIN COOPER and PAUL OAKLEY

I Surrender

Words and Music by
WENDY O'CONNELL

In the Shadow of the Cross

33

Words and Music by
PAUL OAKLEY

1. In the shad-ow of the cross, let ev-'ry-thing fall in-to place a - gain. Je-sus Christ, my Sac - ri - fice,
2. Je-sus Christ, my Per - fect Priest, how You un-der-stand my weak-ness-es. Thank You for Your gift to me.

Let my soul be sat-is-fied.

In my life be glo-ri-fied.

Chords Used in This Song

Intimate Stranger

Guitar capo 3 (D)

Words and Music by
MARTIN SMITH

With awe

35 Investigate

Words and Music by
MARTIN SMITH
and STUART GARRARD

Jesus, Lover of My Soul
(It's All About You)

Capo 1 (A)

Words and Music by
PAUL OAKLEY

Jesus, You Alone

Words and Music by
TIM HUGHES

You will find me long - ing af - ter You.

Chords Used in This Song

Jesus' Blood

38

Words and Music by
MARTIN SMITH

In a relaxed four

1. There's a se - cret I___ must tell___
2. And this se - cret, it___ will run___

of all___ the love I've found.
to the cor - ners of the earth,

And___ it's hid - den in___ my heart,___
where ev - 'ry wo - man, ev - 'ry son___

Je - sus' blood, Je - sus' blood.

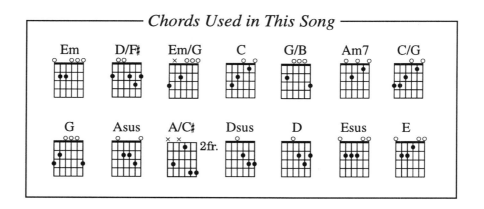

Joy

Words and Music by
JOHN ELLIS

1. I'll love You, Lord, I'll wor-ship You, I'll love You, Lord, al - ways.___ So thank - ful, Lord, You saved my life, You saved my life to - day.___ Let me be a
2. No su - per - man, I'm no he - ro; just a man in Your eyes.___ but through Your Son, I've o - ver - come the fa - ther of all lies.___

D.S. al CODA %

jah.___ 2. I'll

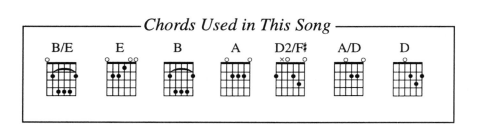

✪ **CODA**

joy to You___ al - ways.___

─── *Chords Used in This Song* ───

B/E   E   B   A   D2/F♯   A/D   D

Justice and Mercy

Words and Music by
MATT REDMAN

Steady four

41

Kindness

Words and Music by
CHRIS TOMLIN, LOUIE GIGLIO
and JESSE REEVES

42

King of This Heart

Words and Music by
MATT REDMAN

Worshipfully

1. Time is too short — to say it's o-kay — to
(2.) stood in the des-ert and thirst-ed for You; — I've

think I can live this way for just an-oth-er day. — So I'll
run through the cit-y, — now I won't let — go. — I'm

search through the night — for the One my heart loves; — won't
throw-ing my-self — on Your mer-cy, O God. — You

stop 'til I've found You. — For, Lord, I need to hold You close. —
say it's all or noth-ing; I'm say-ing, "Je-sus, have it all." —

43

Let My Words Be Few

Capo 1 (G)

Words and Music by
MATT AND BETH REDMAN

44 Light of the World

Words and Music by
MATT REDMAN

45

Make a Joyful Noise/
I Will Not Be Silent

Rhythmically

"Make a Joyful Noise" - Words and Music by Terry Butler

"I Will Not Be Silent" - Words and Music by David Crowder

joy - ful noise—— to the Lord———————— all the earth.——

Make a

Chords Used in This Song

Bm D C G/B A A7sus

G D/F# Em7 C2 Em

Make Your Home in Me

Words and Music by
MICHAEL FRYE and HELEN FRYE

My Glorious

Words and Music by
MARTIN SMITH
and STUART GARRARD

With a strong rock beat

1. The world's shak - ing, with the love of God.
2. Clouds are break - ing, with heav - en's love come to earth.

Great and glo - rious, let the whole earth sing.
Hearts a - wak - 'ning, let the church bells ring.

And all—

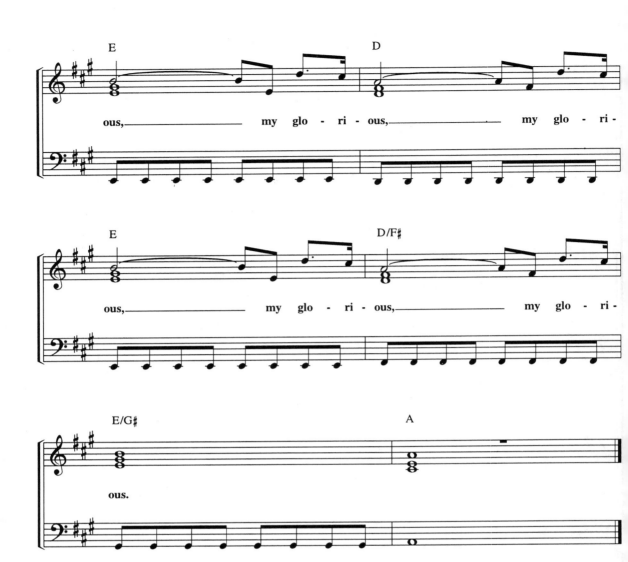

ous,_____ my glo - ri - ous,_____ my glo - ri -

ous,_____ my glo - ri - ous,_____ my glo - ri -

ous.

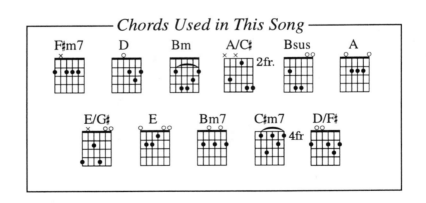

The Noise We Make

Words and Music by
CHRIS TOMLIN and
JESSE REEVES

With a strong beat

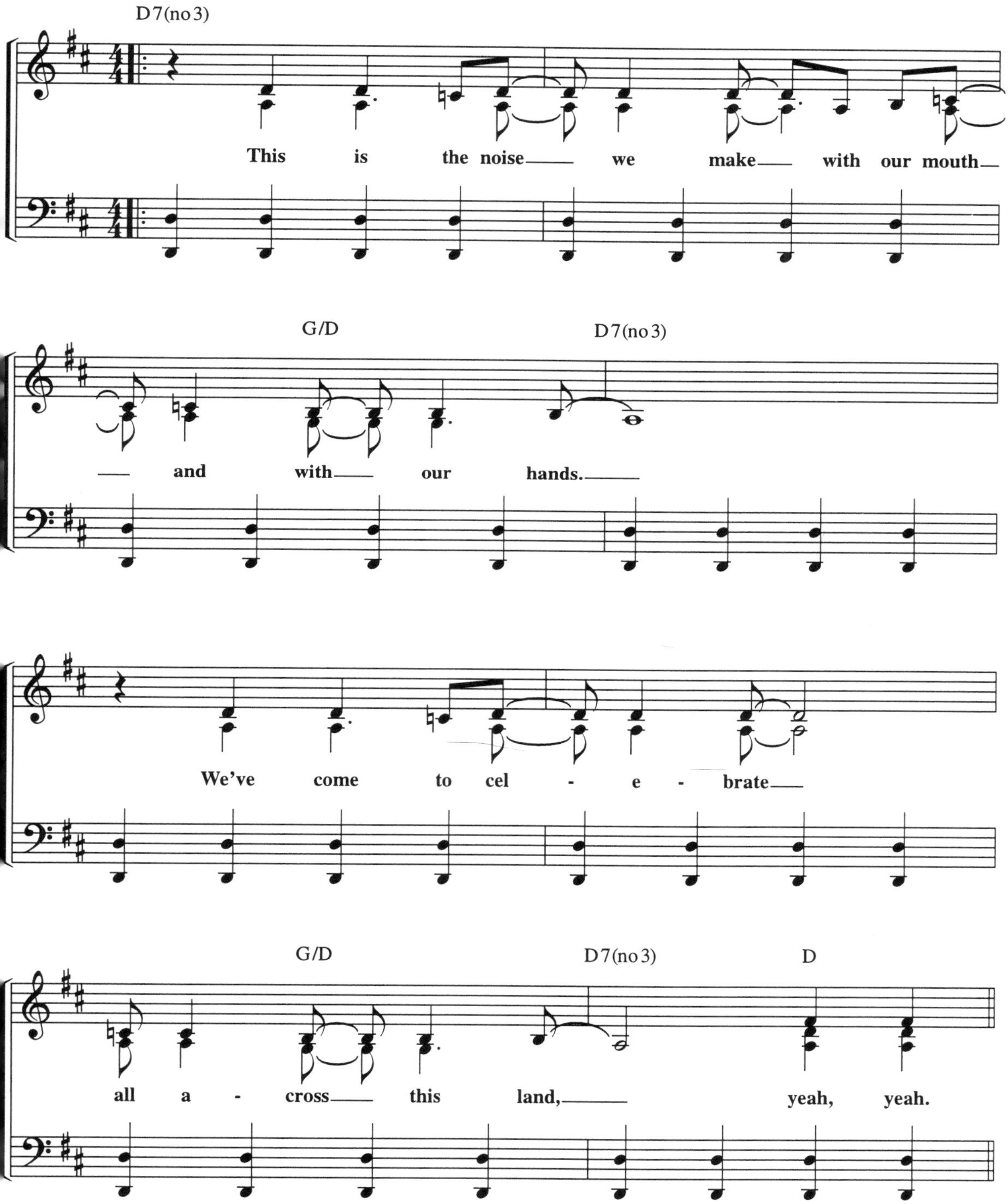
D7(no3)
This is the noise we make with our mouth
G/D
D7(no3)
and with our hands.
We've come to cel - e - brate
G/D
D7(no3)
D
all a - cross this land,
yeah, yeah.

Nothing Is Too Much

Words and Music by
MATT REDMAN and **MIKE PILAVACHI**

50

O Sacred King

Words and Music by
MATT REDMAN

Chords Used in This Song

On and On
(There Will Be No Other)

Words and Music by
MATT REDMAN

51

B 7   A   *D.C. al CODA*

You will have Your praise.

CODA

B 7   A

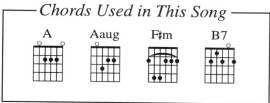

Chords Used in This Song

A   Aaug   F#m   B7

52 Only You

Words and Music by MATT HYAM

I long to know___ You, 'cause on-ly You___ ___ can sa-tis-fy. I long to touch___ ___ You, 'cause on-ly You___ can heal___ my life, heal___ my life.___

Chords Used in This Song

53 Refuge in You

Words and Music by
BRENTON BROWN and PETE JONES

Lord, I have found a re-fuge in You, a hid-ing place where I can en-er in. I meet You there and tell You all my trou-bles, You touch my heart and I am com-fort-ed. I

Chords Used in This Song

G D C2 Em7 C Am7 G/B Dsus

54

Revelation

Words and Music by
MATT REDMAN

Moderate rock beat

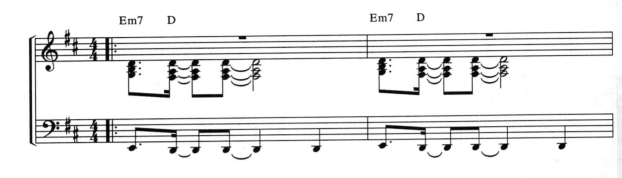

1. ___ We do not wor - ship .... an un - known God,
2. ___ Be - yond all ques - tion, ... You're a mys - ter - y;___
3. Now in part we see You, ... then___ face to face,___

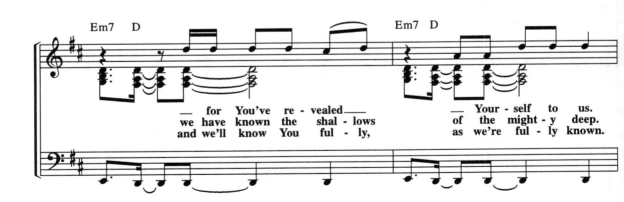

___ for You've re - vealed___ .... Your - self to us.
we have known the shal - lows .... of the might - y deep.
and we'll know You ful - ly, ... as we're ful - ly known.

The Rhythm of Heaven

55

Words and Music by
PETER ECKLEY and NIGEL HEMMING

here   'cause we heard Your— Spir-it's call;   now the cur-tain— has been

torn,   as we wor-ship— we are freed.   2. Can you

freed.   *D.S. al Fine*   freed.—   *Fine*

— Chords Used in This Song —

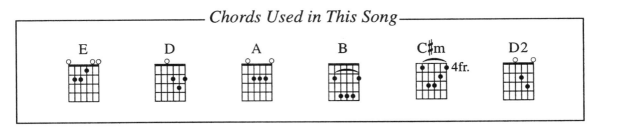

E   D   A   B   C♯m   D2

56

Salvation

Words and Music by
CHARLIE HALL

and   cry———— out   to   You.

Chords Used in This Song

57
Shout to the North

Words and Music by
MARTIN SMITH

With praise

Sing Like the Saved

Words and Music by
MATT REDMAN

Joyfully

1. We're gon - na sing like the saved,_____
2. A joy - ful noise we will make,_____
3. You put this joy in our hearts,_____
4. We're gon - na dance like the saved,_____

we're gon - na sing like the saved,_____
a joy - ful noise we will make,_____
You put this joy in our hearts,_____
we're gon - na dance like the saved,_____

we're gon - na sing like the saved,_____
a joy - ful noise we will make,_____
You put this joy in our hearts,_____
we're gon - na dance like the saved,_____

Surrender

Words and Music by
MARC JAMES

all___ to you   And

I ___   sur - ren - der   All   to you,___

all___ to you

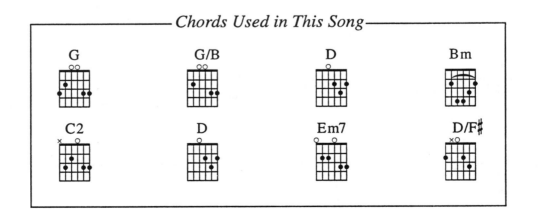

Chords Used in This Song

G   G/B   D   Bm

C2   D   Em7   D/F#

60

Take the World but Give Me Jesus

Words and Music by
MATT REDMAN

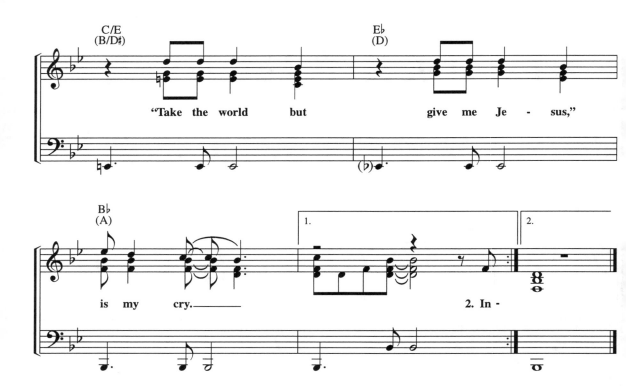

"Take the world but give me Je - sus," is my cry._____ 2. In -

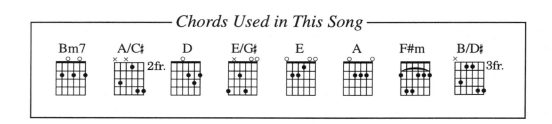

Thank You for the Blood

61

Words and Music by
MATT REDMAN

With praise

Thank You, thank You for the blood that You shed,_____

Stand-ing in its bless-ing, we sing_____ these free - dom songs._____

Thank You, thank You for the bat - tle You won._____

Stand-ing in Your vict-'ry, we sing_____ sal - va - tion songs,_____ we sing_____

62 There's No One Like Our God

Words and Music by
VICKY BEECHING and STEVE MITCHINSON

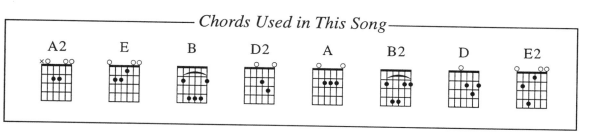

Chords Used in This Song

A2   E   B   D2   A   B2   D   E2

We Bow Down at Your Throne

Words and Music by
JESS HUMPHRIES

In an easy four

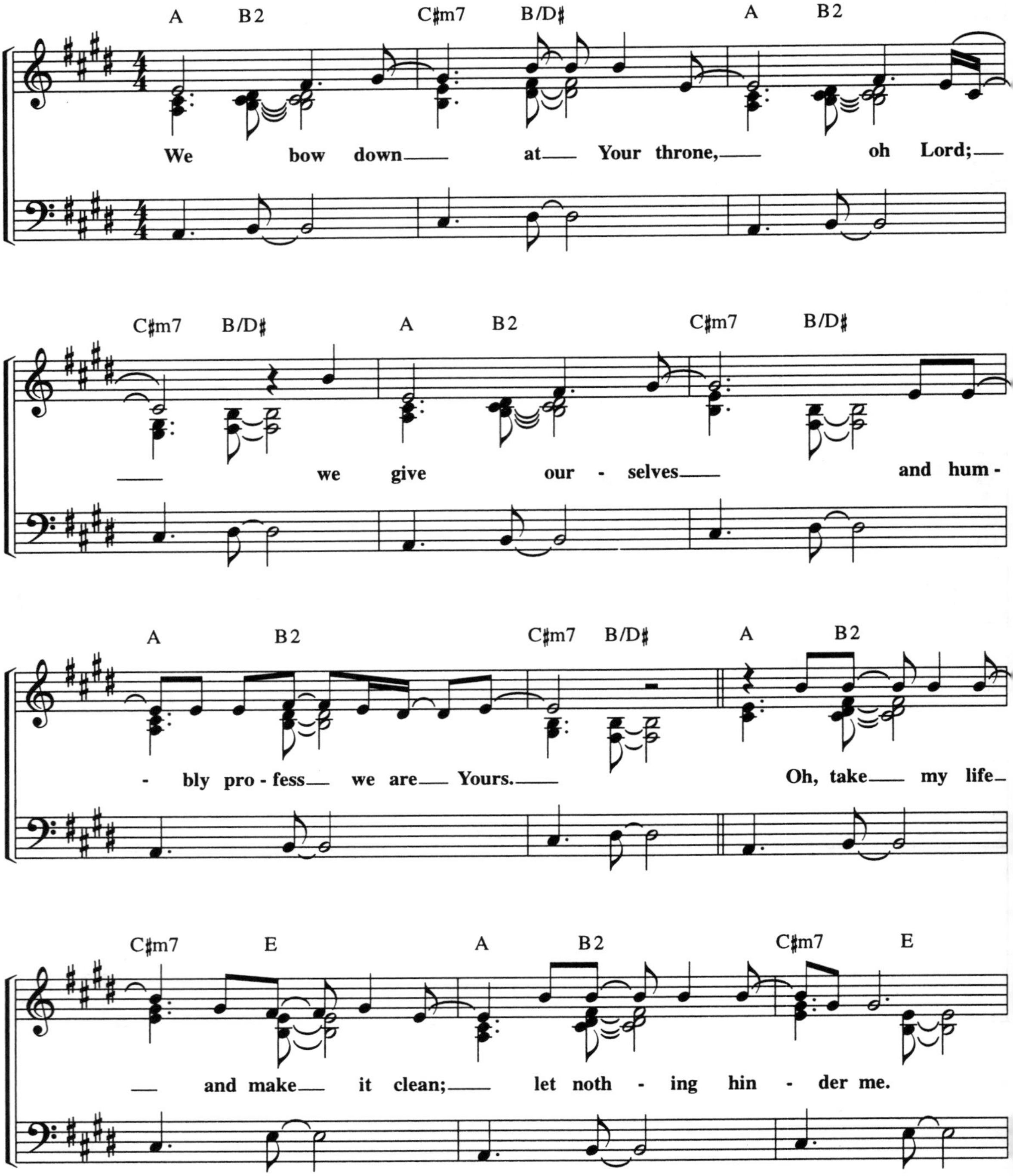
A B2 C♯m7 B/D♯ A B2
We bow down at Your throne, oh Lord;
C♯m7 B/D♯ A B2 C♯m7 B/D♯
we give our - selves and hum -
A B2 C♯m7 B/D♯ A B2
- bly pro - fess we are Yours. Oh, take my life
C♯m7 E A B2 C♯m7 E
and make it clean; let noth - ing hin - der me.

64

We Fall Down

Words and Music by
CHRIS TOMLIN

Capo 2 (D)

Optional African lyrics:

Re o bama, re I koba naong tsa go Jesu. Lo lorato le legolo naong tsa go Jesu.

O boitshepo, boitshepo, O boitshepo, boitshepo, O boitshepo, boitshepo, O kwana.

65
We Will Be Together

Words and Music by
SHARON HEAP

We will be to-

ge - ther___

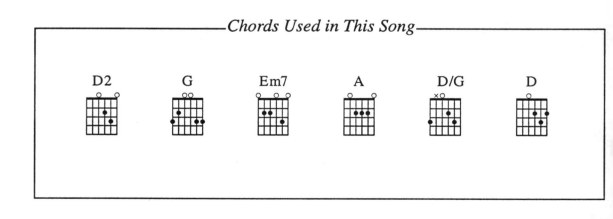

Chords Used in This Song

D2   G   Em7   A   D/G   D

What a Child Is Meant to Be

Words and Music by
KATHRYN SCOTT

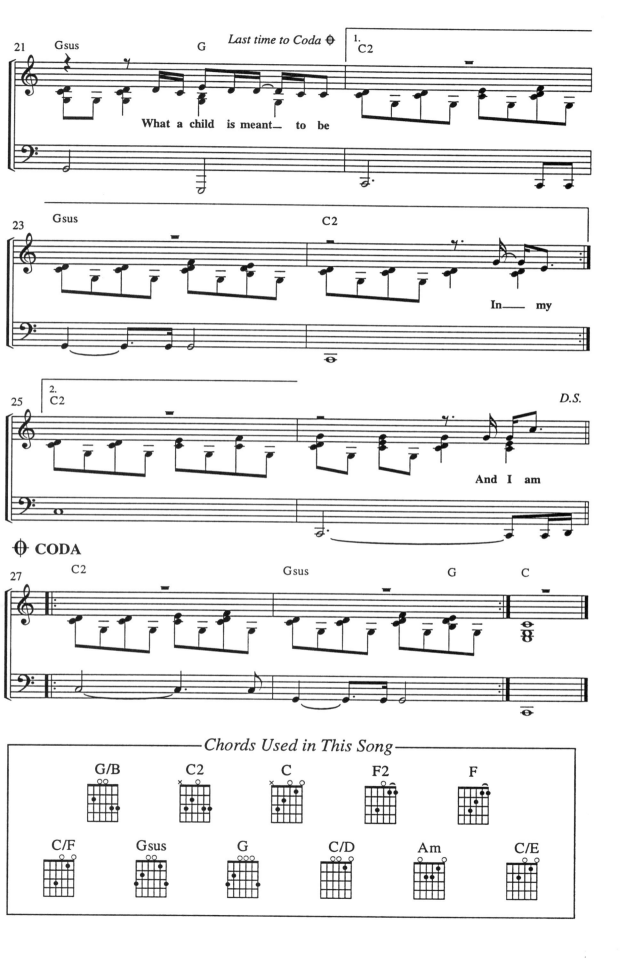

67 What Would I Have Done?

Words and Music by
MARTIN SMITH

-sus?_____

Em/D   D

Em/D   D

2.   D

if   it   was - n't___   for   Je - sus?____

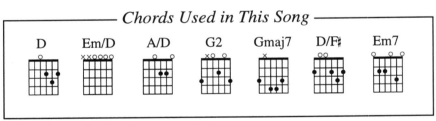

— *Chords Used in This Song* —

D   Em/D   A/D   G2   Gmaj7   D/F♯   Em7

When You Call My Name

68

Words and Music by
BRIAN DOERKSEN and STEVE MITCHINSON

There's a hun-ger in this wil-der-ness
I am seek-ing true i-den-ti-ty

For your re-ve-la-tion
In the light of your pre-sence

To hear the words of life that strength-en me
I am long-ing to know how you see me

Come and show what you've pre-pared for me
In the time that you have giv-en me,

With You

Words and Music by
BRENTON BROWN

70
The Years Go By

Words and Music by
MARTIN SMITH

Chords Used in This Song

You Are a Holy God

Words and Music by
BRIAN DUANE and KATHRYN SCOTT

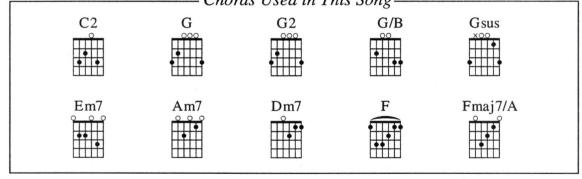

Chords Used in This Song

You Are My King

Words and Music by
BRIAN DOERKSEN

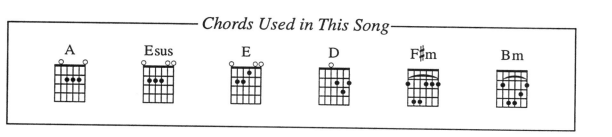

Chords Used in This Song

73

You Are My King
(Amazing Love)

Words and Music by
BILLY JAMES FOOTE

I'm for-giv-en be-cause You were for-sak-en.

I'm ac-cept-ed; You were con-demned.

I'm a-live and well, Your Spir-it is with-in me be-

cause You died and rose a-gain.

You are my King,

You are my King. Je - sus, You are my

D.C. al Coda

King. Je - sus, You are my King.

✛ CODA

Bsus   B   A   B   E

In all I do I hon-or You.

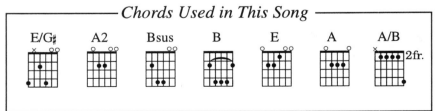

Chords Used in This Song

E/G♯   A2   Bsus   B   E   A   A/B

You Led Me to the Cross

74

Words and Music by
MATT REDMAN

Steady four, with emotion

1. You led me to the cross,_____ and I saw the
2. And there's an emp-ty tomb_____ that tells me of Your

face of mer-cy_____ in that_____ place of love._____
res-ur-rec-tion_____ and my_____ life in You._____

You o-pened up my eyes_____ to be-lieve Your
The stone lies rolled a-way,_____ noth-ing but those

sweet sal-va-tion_____ where I'd_____ been so blind._____
fold-ed grave clothes_____ where Your_____ bod-y lay._____

Sav - ior, teach____ me of the cross;____

I won't__ for - get____ the love,____

I won't__ for - get____ the love____ You've_____ shown.____

Chords Used in This Song

A   E/G♯   F♯m7   D   B7/D♯   E

75

You Must Increase

**Words and Music by
MATT REDMAN**

Copyright © 2000 Kingsway's Thankyou Music.
Administered in the Western Hemisphere by EMI Christian Music Publishing,
P.O. Box 5085, Brentwood, TN 37204-5085.
All rights reserved. Used by permission.

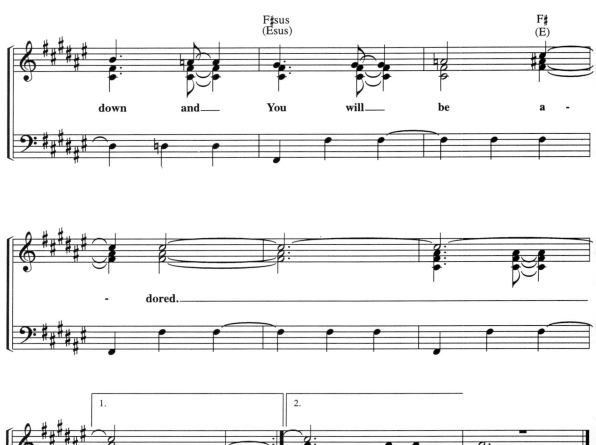

F#sus
(Esus)

F#
(E)

down   and——   You   will——   be   a -

- dored._____

1.

2.

—— I——— ——

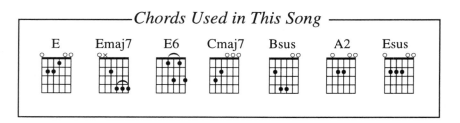

Chords Used in This Song

E   Emaj7   E6   Cmaj7   Bsus   A2   Esus

You Opened Up My Eyes

Words and Music by
MARTIN LAYZELL

Your Name Is Holy

Words and Music by
BRIAN DOERKSEN

in Your ho - ly name.

Your name is ho - ly.

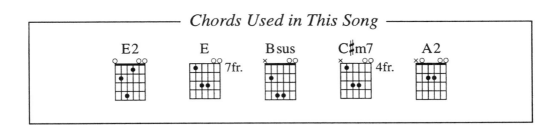

(Appendix A)

Index of Songs by Key

Mid-tempo

Slow Mid-tempo

Slow

(Appendix C)

Index of Songs by Project

Passion: Road To OneDay

Live and Unreserved

Matt Redman: The Father's Song

Passion: OneDay Live

Delirious?: Glo

Vineyard UK: Hungry

Vineyard UK: Surrender

Additional Songs